'Mad' Mike Hughes:
The Tell-All Tale
Incredible Stunts Publications

Copyright 2018

.

Dedicated to the human spirit, to JoJo, my cat and friend, that died in 1998, and Alex, my cat and friend, that died in 2016.

Preface

March 24, 2018

MOJAVE DESERT

"This thing wants to kill you ten different ways," Michael Hughes, said of his homemade steam-powered rocket, a veritable bomb, shortly before ascending the ladder and climbing into the cockpit. "It will kill you in a heartbeat."

Is "Mad" Mike Hughes more renaissance man or mad man? Does he really think the world is flat, or is he just challenging convention?

Here is Mad Mike Hughes in the Liberty Rocket, seconds before the launch which was just one step in a more ambitious "space jump".

There was no countdown. There was no predicting what would come next. After months of ups and downs, cancellations, delays, and distractions, it was finally ready to happen.

But wait a minute, you might ask: wasn't this the same self-taught rocket scientist who said he didn't believe in science and that he believes the world could, in fact, be flat?

Yes, but that's not all he said. In its full context his actual statement was:

"I don't believe in science; I know about aerodynamics and fluid dynamics and how things move through the air, about the certain size of rocket nozzles, and thrust. But that's not science, that's just a formula. There's no difference between science and science fiction."

And this rocket launch is just part of a bigger plan which would end with Mike eventually proving, or disproving, the roundness of the planet.

"Do I believe the Earth is shaped like a Frisbee? I believe it is," he said."Do I know for sure? No. That's why I want to go up in space."

But before we get into how that launch turned out, let's learn about Mike, in his own words, and by his own actions. He has said he intends to make multiple rocket journeys, culminating in a flight to outer space, where he believes he will be able to take a picture of the entire Earth as a "flat disk".

Does he live up to the title King of The Daredevils? Read on and decide for yourself.

Table of Contents

AT THE STARTING LINE

"Mad" Mike Hughes got his start in NASCAR in the winter of 1986. As he tells it:

I'd been around racing my whole life. My Dad was a racer. I went to my first car race at two months of age.

In Oklahoma City, my dad worked in a body shop and raced on the weekends. He actually turned professional in 1960. His car ran a Grand National race, which was Winston Cup or the Monster Cup Series, or whatever the hell they're calling it now. It used to be called Grand National Series.

He did one race in Atlanta with his own car and then the next year he went down the circuit for three years.

He traveled and sometimes we travel with my brother and my mom to the races and I didn't know where I was at half the time, you know, I don't know if I was in that Des Moines, Iowa or St Paul, Minnesota or a Shreveport , Louisiana or next to my hometown in Oklahoma City.

I had no idea know. We traveled around: he raced the county fair circuit, these cars from Shreveport, Louisiana all the way to St Paul, Minnesota.

We hit every county fair, you know, that was big back in the fifties and sixties. That's what you did. Motorcycles and cars. It was just a huge circuit.

I remember getting close to the racetrack. I could smell burning rear end grease and would know I was as close to the race track. I still remember that.

But my dad came out of the circuit 63. I think he was tired of traveling, really didn't think the money was that great anymore, and went back to work in a body shop in Oklahoma City and started racing on the weekends.

I would watch him working for the countless hours he or he would do it, you know, especially when he was not on the races. He'd have to have a regular job back home and then he'd come home and work on a race car, build one or something and, you know, it's just continuous work.

For people as that do this or have done it, it's just consuming. It consumes your life.

You got no time for anything else and it just eats at relationships like termites to wood

On my first Nascar job in 86, I worked New Year's Eve until 11:30 at night and I know my girlfriend was all ready to go out. My girlfriend was already dressed and ready to go out for New Year's Eve.

I got home. I said, I am just, I can't do it. I'm wore out, you know what I mean? I've worked on Christmas day before I have all that stuff, you know.

It's just, it's just an endless cycle.

Any major injuries in racing motorcycle or Nascar?

I didn't start breaking my back until I got into doing stunts and stuff like that. But as far as the motorcycle racing, I broke several bones. that's just part of the deal.

There's some people go to whole career and maybe don't break anything or some people that just break, you know, several bones or several at once or whatever.

I remember after crashing and laying on some racetrack thinking that my back was broke. I looked down at my feet to make sure they were pointing the right direction

And I remember my second pro race, someone got killed on the front straightaway. I had a fifteen-year-old kid with me, he was helping me the race and he, he turned white. This is what can happen. I've seen three people killed at racetracks but that's part of the deal.

Mike's introduction to stunts:

I had a motorcycle racing buddy, a guy named Steve Hunt. You can actually look them up on the Internet. He was a motorcycle jumper back the mid-Seventies. A lot of people were doing it.

Very few people were making money. Just Evel Knievel and I think that one girl, Debbie Evans and Gary Wells may have made a little money at it, but most people would just pay their gas with it.

That's what Steve was doing. He got hurt really bad in Tulsa, Oklahoma. I wasn't there that night. I saw Evel Knievel jumped twice. A lot of people was doing it and it just never really crossed my mind to do it. Honestly, it just didn't, until I got to be a limousine driver in Vegas.

I dreamed up and after working on it, it eventually it into some kind of a career, I guess. And then one night I thought, what can I do to break away and, and be the top stuntman in the world, the top daredevil?

I thought, man, I'm going to recreate the Evel Knievel state and rocket jump. That's the Holy Grail of stunts. The Holy Grail. Everyone talked about it. People tried to build rockets. People today we're going to do it. And no one else did it in this crazy thing is, when Knievel did it in 74.

There were 1 million people that paid to watch Knievel at the Snake River September 8, 1974, and to think I would be the next guy to do this !!

What are the odds of that?

RACING IN CIRCLES

(Mike's Winston West race car testing at California Speedway 2002)

Before rocketry became his passion, Michael Hughes was involved with NASCAR where he established himself as something of an innovator. It was during this time that he became an aerodynamics specialist.

In contrast to racing, rocketry was a relief from what he described as the burnout that came with NASCAR.

"Well, I just got burnt out on it. It's a lot of work. You're traveling with guys. It's just endless. You are always behind. You're never caught up. The older I got, the more I didn't want to just do it.

"I wanted to drive or maybe own a team or something. I didn't want to be a worker bee. That's all you are. You're a worker bee. That sport right there, NASCAR, has absolutely bankrupted and ruined families and individuals by the hundreds."

Much of racing has changed since Mike was in it, and in his view, not for the better. "The whole sport has changed since I have left it. They use lasers to line the cars up, now, and overall, it just turned into a homogenous sport."

"They made it like golf is what they've done."

"They've ruined the sport. There are no more personalities. I was tired of seeing those punk little kids show up with daddy's money racing. I just didn't really want to be around it anymore because I just saw it start going downhill.

That said, Mike made his mark. He even had a car in the Days of Thunder movie and it went up on the front page in National Enquirer: "I built it in January 1990."

He was also the first to vinyl wrap a NASCAR car.

"I was the first guy to vinyl wrap a NASCAR car, which revolutionized the sport. People still use it. They will always use it. I'm the first guy that did it. I've got the story to prove it and the car that was first wrapped was actually destroyed here on the West Coast in a crash."

This wasn't his only innovation in the sport. He also:

"...designed the first prototype carbon fiber air cleaner that they still use today. I'm a pretty innovative guy.

I believe that no other man has introduced as many revolutionary and innovative ideas as I have in NASCAR."

THE SKY LIMO

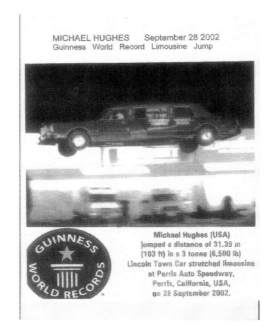

MICHAEL HUGHES   September 28 2002
Guinness World Record Limousine Jump

Michael Hughes (USA)
jumped a distance of 31.39 m
(103 ft) in a 3 tonne (6,500 lb)
Lincoln Town Car stretched limousine
at Perris Auto Speedway,
Perris, California, USA,
on 28 September 2002.

28 SEPTEMBER 2002

Michael Hughes (USA) jumped a distance of 31.39 m (103 ft) in a 3 tonne (6,500 lb) Lincoln Town Car stretched limousine at Perris Auto Speedway, Perris, California, USA

Hughes has widely been referred to (with good reason) as "the world's most famous limo driver."

How he got his start in Limousine jumping:

"This was my first foray really into stunts. It was a Cadillac. It was something I had bought somewhere in someone's backyard in Vegas. I jumped it twice. Someone gave me one in Sacramento. That's when I set the record in Paris Speedway back in 2002. Since then, someone broke my record I believe in 2016. They jumped like one-hundred and forty-seven feet."

Mike's record was one hundred and three feet, but he isn't sure if that's accurate:

"Again, see, They are supposed to measure from. the back wheel. They might have measured from the front wheel. You don't know. See what I mean? You don't know what these characters have done."

There is a lot of preparation that goes into setting up a limousine to make a stunt jump. And there is no second chance, as Mike explains:

"It stiffens up the suspension. I chained the rear end where it wouldn't rebound coming off the ramp, but really, you just need a really good seat that takes the shock and just set the suspension up.

"You've got three inches of travel and it hits and bottoms out. You really need like a 100-foot long ramp to a 10-degree angle, but I never had the money for all that stuff. Breaking my back twice doing it."

About setting distance records for Limousine jumping:

"I was the first one to do it. Then I set a record and then a couple of people tried it. One guy claimed he broke my record. Then I found out he measured from the front end instead of the rear of the car, which is, you know, another 17 or 18 feet or whatever it was.

"So like I said before, you gotta watch how these guys do it, do this and what you're measuring from and you know, it's like with the motorcycle jumps, you measure from them back, where it lands. So same with the car and a limousine. That's a big difference between the front and rear of a car, you know?

"But some guy did break it. I know of in 2016. He was like 143 feet or something. It went quite a ways in Chicago, but it was a big production. He, he probably spent more on power techniques now I ever did on any limousine. It was a big production.

"And can I beat it the out? Of course. I'm sure I have forgotten more about suspension than this guy will ever know. You know, unless I get paid, if it's not going to pay, there's no need to. Just to say I'd beat guy's record that beat mine, who cares? You don't know the guy's name, but you know my name, from the rocket jump."

On one of those jumps, the one in San Bernardino, was on the Jimmy Kimmel Show:

"This became the biggest news story in L.A. for like three days. I don't know how many times it aired. It led to me being on Jimmy Kimmel Live."

March 2004 Las Vegas Life story Driven To Fame

SELF-TAUGHT ROCKET SCIENTIST

Michael Hughes is one man, doing things on his own. As a self-taught rocket scientist, he had to learn on his own, spending "thousands of hours" reading up on rockets, as he put it, until "the Internet came along, and I didn't have to go to the library anymore."

He learned what he needed to and built his own steam-powered rocket, a thermal rocket which uses heated water held in a vessel at a high temperature which then escapes as steam through the nozzle to produce thrust.

"You're unleashing the devil with this thing. That's the only way to describe it," he told ArsTechnica.com before his scheduled Palo Duro Canyon jump.

Mad Mike's Sky Limo rocket was designed to fire for about four seconds with an initial thrust of approximately 4,000 pounds, which then increases to about 7,000 pounds at its peak with a G-force of 4-7.

"I've had to do this on my own dime," he said. "The only way I can do this is by making everything myself. Evel Knievel spent $600,000 on his rocket. I make $15 an hour. You do the math."

In addition to learning how to build the rocket came the issue of where. As Mike described it:

"One of the drawbacks of this is when you go somewhere, no one wants you to build on their property, okay? So if you're gonna have to build a big old long ramp, that may turn someone off.

"I'd like to have done it mobile with a semi-truck with a 53 foot trailer on the back of it so it would've been safer, heavier, and then you could just make the ramp go up with a push of a button like a dump truck, that's the way to do these things. But I never had the money to do it, to do it properly.

"That's how you ought to do these things, on the back of a semi where nothing's gonna move and you just hit a button and the dump truck Ram just pushes it up to the right angle and then you fire.

Wow, okay. Now, what got you into steam-powered rockets in the first place?

That's just the simplest way to do this thing. You know, the fuel doesn't cost anything. The problem is when this thing is heated up, the energy is already created. It's waiting to fire. That's the problem, you're sitting on top of a bomb and it's ready to go."

This Palo Duro jump didn't happen as scheduled, but this didn't stop Mike from moving forward, even as he planned for his "space jump", which involves ballooning up to 20,000 feet before launching all the way up to the Karman line, or approximately 62 miles above the earth's surface. High enough to see the curve, or lack thereof, of planet Earth.

On March 30, 2016, Hughes told Ars Technica about some very sketchy plans to take "a balloon up to 20,000 feet or so with a rocket strapped to his shoulders, releasing the balloon, and flying all the way to 62 miles above the planet, into outer space, before coming back to Earth."[8] Balloon-rocket hybrids, while technically feasible, have both substantial limitations and complications.

MEET THE FLAT EARTHERS

In June of 2017, a massive advertisement went up right outside the Philadelphia International Airport. It was for the most controversial topic in the world: Flat Earth theory.

The first of many such billboards, the "Research Flat Earth" billboard on I-76 was purchased by the Infinite Plane Society, a group of truthers exploring the notion that the Earth's shape is not a foregone conclusion.

Thanks to a viral CBS news story in which a Flat Earther declared the International Space Station to be "fake'", the moon landings "hoaxes", the "Research Flat Earth" billboard campaign gained the attention of millions, including "Mad" Mike Hughes.

Flat Earth believers flocked in from across the country to have their selfies taken with it.

Notably Karlee Sunshine, whose video showed up in the Youtube feed of Mad Mike Hughes, who had already questioned the shape of the world and whether it moves around the sun or vice versa.

He knew the rocket would make an excellent billboard and would gain far more attention to the idea and to his own stunt than a regular old sign.

He called into the Infinite Plane Society live stream to introduce his plan to like-minded individuals. This time, he aimed to launch himself on a mile-long flight over the Mojave Desert, a veritable steam-powered billboard.

"Yeah. My name is Mad Mike Hughes. I'm a daredevil here in southern California and a limo driver, a former NASCAR crew chief, and former professional motorcycle racer. So I've been around the world basically and some days it feels like it, like today.

"Yeah, you know, basically I was kind of known as the world's most famous limousine driver and I got involved with NASCAR and I revolutionized that sport.

I set the record for the longest limousine jump and did three or four jumps and I set the record in Paris, California, broke my back for the second time and I'm thinking, "This is not paying very well." And I'm thinking, "I'm going to do the Evil Knievel rocket jump."

Without knowing anything about rockets and so many years later I finally do a jump, and jump a quarter mile and I'm getting ready to jump a mile in Amboy, California, within 45 to 60 days. I'm going to jump the whole town of Amboy. We're going to launch 300 foot from Route 66 and it's going to be the longest jump of all time and probably the greatest daredevil stunt of all time because I'm going to launch this rocket from a mobile rocket launcher, which I'm the only man in the world that has one. I built it just like my rocket, so it's quite an endeavor.

And you said in 45 to 60 days?

Oh yes, yeah. The rocket's in the back of the ramp right now. In fact, I'm working on it and I'm still perfecting some of the ramp because it's got to ... You know it's 60 foot long. It's in a motorhome which as you lift it up it's just a ... It's quite an endeavor and plus making the rocket where you can lift in this thing because it's five to seven G's and this thing's going to hit 500 miles an hour. It's going to go to about 1500 feet altitude and jump a mile. So, this is serious. This is no joke. The last time I jumped I took a hit of 20 G's when I landed. I was in a walker for a couple weeks, so this thing can take your life.

You know, I'm just one guy and honestly, I'm not a tech guy which is really a bad deal for me because I don't really know how to negotiate all the stuff for all this Twitter and Facebook and whatever. I'm a nuts and bolts guy. I know to build things to make it happen. I study. I teach myself things and I put small pieces together to make the large picture and that's what I did with this rocket and that's what I did with NASCAR and that's how I understand things, but this whole tech thing is ... I'm really behind the eight ball on it.

Now, this is incredible. We just watched a video of your rocket jump. This is amazing. I'm going to replay that. That is just something. Yeah. Daredevil is correct. This is incredible.

So, basically, I am the only gentleman in the history of mankind to design, build, and launch themselves in their own rocket.

That's how I learned about you, from the billboard. I've been a believer ... Almost a year ... I researched it for several months. In between doing everything else, you know you still have to try to make a living and everything and all that kind of stuff and this rocket just actually eats up a lot of my time. But when I'm not doing that, I research things. I mean everything. And this is why I know a lot about the background of NASA, Elon Musk, you know ... If you want to talk about NASA and talk about that ... A lot of things.

But you know, I'm not a stock market guy. I don't believe in it. I don't believe in banking. You know, I believe in the real things. The problems are people growing up nowadays don't the difference between CGI and what is real.

Right, right. And you know, what's interesting about this conversation is for months now, I've been calling out astronauts as doing a form of stolen valor because what you're doing ... Getting launched at seven G's of force ... That's valor. That's going and putting yourself on the line. You're not acting.

Yeah. You're rolling the dice. I rolled the dice that day because I thought I had 30% chance of surviving because the parachutes were 20 years old and the other one was 23 years old and one of them didn't even open when I landed.

And that's when you took the 20 G's, okay.

Yeah. It was a scary moment because I was coming ... I'd never parachuted before, skydiving. I was coming down to fast and I'm just stuck in this thing. There's nothing I could do. And luckily I built the nose where it would take a 45 to 50 mile per hour hit, which is what saved my life. I mean from my background in NASCAR and building things is what saved my life that afternoon.

That is just amazing and yeah, hey we're all going to be following what you're doing, especially you're next jump. We're going to be looking with great interest. And what does it take to get a message on the side of your rocket?

Well, you know, we're kind of looking for a main sponsor for this thing. Of course, it's a big area. It's like 22 inches by eight-foot long white stuff in the middle of the rocket and I'm trying to find the right thing for that and I'm a believer in the flat earth but anyway, to get back to the NASA thing. You know, most of those NASA astronauts are Freemasons so John Glen, and Neil Armstrong, you know, they're Freemasons. So when you understand that, then you kinda understand that there can be some deception there.

But what really turned me on NASA was learning about Thomas Ronald Baron, who was killed in April '67 after a 500-page report to NASA explaining how disarrayed the old program was. He died- A train hit his car, killing his wife, him, and his stepdaughter. Six days after that and the 500-page report hasn't even been sent. So you tell me what's going on.

Yeah, so he was probably an honest guy. Wasn't in the club, wasn't gonna swear-

But see they don't want that in the corporate world. It's just like Joe Bannister who went to IRS and said "This is not right, I researched it for two and a half years, and there's no legitimate taxes. And he says "Okay, here's the walking papers." And they took him to court, tried to send him to prison. So that's how that whole deal works.

Gus Grissom who died on the launchpad there with two other astronauts used to hang lemons inside one of the spacecraft. So it would ever make it to the moon, it's impossible. He's one of the astronauts who died in that fire. And I still think he was murdered.

What do you think? Richard Branson with Virgin Galactic, you know had the New Mexico. He had the state pay 150 million dollars for space for it, and he's not gonna use it. How come he's not at court or in jail over that?

So you know, and just to let you know, I have a friend of mine, and myself have a plan to put me 62 miles up into space as an individual. We have all the components. 62 miles up, which is the real Kármán line, the edge of space, to prove once and for all the earth is flat. I think I'll prove anything, okay? It will shut the door on all this other- This ball earth, and the because there are 1.8 million dollars, it can be done within 6-9 months.

Real life, I've lost more people than Elon Musk has in a rocket.

And so did you see the Research Flat Earth billboard in person, or just online?

No, no. I live in southern California, so I saw it on the Internet. I was just researching Flat Earth videos, and then this came up because there are several people- I can't give you the names, I just follow 'em, and you know, you don't have to believe everything everybody says in this whole movement.

You put all these collective things together, and you draw your own conclusions. Okay? But most people don't do that now. They have a collective reasoning. It's what they have. Which is what their family thinks, their husband thinks, their job, people that work think. They don't have their own individual thoughts.

Now think about this, sir. Seven years after 9/11 people in this country voted for a person with a Muslim name. Barack Hussein Obama. Now you figure that one out.

Everything's an act. All the stuff with this defacto government is an act.

We were all declared enemies of the state in 1933 by Franklin Delano Roosevelt when he called in all the gold. So the last thing you wanna be is a United States citizen. That's the very last thing you wanna be. And it's absolutely bizarre, and I use that word every day. So yeah, you know I took all this knowledge, and I draw my conclusions. And you know, we're told things when we're young. It's like okay, the sun is 93 million miles away. "Okay, that's cool." You're 8 years old, what the hell do you know? You know? And then the moon is 238,000 miles away. "Okay." And we live in this big conglomerate thing, and "Okay." And you think "This isn't even possible." Our world is not spinning at 1,038 miles an hour at the equator. It ain't happening. But you're told things and you just accept them, and you think "Okay, that's just the way it is."

And that is what happened with our lives about everything. Because history's getting rewritten.Yes. And this is the king of the deceptions. This is it. And once this domino falls and more people come to this side, then everything else, the dominoes start to fall, and this is what the elite are afraid of.

Yeah, this is gonna be a huge media advantage, and the thing is, this rocket will stay in its place from now on.

It's gonna be built, and it will be on display in Las Vegas, and it will never be painted. It'll go up and down Hollywood Boulevard, a friend of mine owns a network there, and right down Hollywood and Vine. I mean parked there one day, probably about 2 months. So the amount of media cannot even be bought, what this is gonna bring from now on, because this rocket will never ever be touched. The logos stay on forever. And then hopefully that'll be a base for this space launch maybe later this year.

Well, thank you for joining us, Mike.

It's my pleasure. I just love to be around intelligent people, and you know the story, I'm not a tech guy, I just can't discuss all this, everything about this live stream and what- You know I'm just not well versed in it. So I'm just a nuts and bolts guy, but I'm

61 years old, and that's kind of the generation I grew up in. You know, I built things.

Yeah, then you gotta man up and get in it. You know? So that's- I just cannot believe in today, I just- You know, all you gotta do, is when you go somewhere is look around at the people. They look medicated, they look disheveled, they look like their clothes need to be pressed, you know? It's just bizarre. And you think "Go, what's causing all this? It can't be just television." Is it the medication? Is it? I don't know.

"Oh yeah, and I don't follow- I've never watched a Star Wars, I've been to the movies once in ten years. I don't support these people. I don't care about Tom Cruise or George Clooney, or what Matt Damon thinks. I don't care, because it is irrelevant.

Yeah, it's my pleasure man. Everyone just hang in there, I know you get rattled by people who think you're a nut, and they just- 'Cause people don't understand what they don't understand. And that's just the simplest way I can put it. You don't know what you don't know."

And thus, the Flat Earth community had a new champion.

SNAKE RIVER FIASCO

Part of being a daredevil is getting around bureaucratic red-tape. Several launches were scrapped, delayed, and canceled, all of which made the final launch all the more impressive of a feat.

Unlawful acts of the local and state officials in Idaho got in the way of Mad Mike's scheduled jump where Evel Knievel had attempted to jump Idaho's immense Snake River Canyon. And when the stunt was completed successfully by Eddie Braun, the "Daredevil" had been taken out of it, according to "Mad" Mike Hughes.

As he describes it:

"Yeah. That's a story in itself. That basically turned into criminal activity by the state and by the city council of Twin Falls, Idaho.

In fact, I was so pissed off I called the Attorney General of the state of Idaho.

I said, "The people at the land department that are putting this thing up for bid. They cannot do that."

They said, "If you take us to court, I'm going to have to defend them."

I said, "Wait a second. You would defend them, knowing they are breaking the law and not following their guidelines on leasing public land?"

See, that's what happens. You get these legal departments involved and it's like taking a crap in the middle of someone's swimming pool.

Yeah. The learning curve is pretty severe during this, okay? It really is, especially when there's no money. If you haven't tested it before, you had to test it before. If you've got one to two million dollars to throw at something, it makes it easier, especially if you already launched one or two rockets.

And then you've got a remote from the ground in case it doesn't open.

All that stuff takes the daredevil part out of it. Now it's just a stunt. It's been rehearsed, which is what Eddie Braun was at the Snake River. He spent $1.6 million. I beat him to the punch by two and a half years.

The sad thing is if everyone hadn't acted criminal at the Twin Falls, I would have been the one that done that on the 39th anniversary.

And basically ABC, they never gave me money up front. We were talking about a reality show. A couple jumps, they were gonna put me on 20/20 and Good Morning America after I launched. John Green was with 20/20. I was in discussion with him and Morgan Zalkin from good morning America about what ABC was interested in.

They knew I was at the Winkelman Arizona launch site because John Green from 20/20 was actually was at the Winkelman Arizona launch site with his mother a couple of months before I eventually launched

Then after I launched, a friend of mine sends them the footage and then they didn't wanna do nothing with it.

Above: Hughes taking off in his first manned rocket on January 30, 2014, and flew 1,374 feet (419 m) in just over one minute over Winkelman, Arizona.

I go, "Well, what's up? We had this agreement or I would let other networks cover this thing and send it out. Pretty soon it got to be old news and then no one really wanted the thing.

So it really, ABC screwed me in a way that is ... they acted criminally also. If it was the other way around, man, they'd have me in court before I knew it, you know what I mean? So basically I did not let anyone else shoot it or be there and we didn't send the footage to anyone else, 'cause ABC was gonna take care of me and make me a hero, and they did nothing.

ABC was acting like whores at the Twin Falls ... I never went to Twin Falls with it, Snake River Canyon. I talked to the city council and this and that, sent some information, and they just acted like whores.

DEATH AND ROCKETS

Mike describes the dangerous nature of rocketry:

"I was going to jump about six months before the Snake River one, but we had a rocket break loose sitting on the launch ramp. It went sixth-tenths of a mile, hitting the ground going about 275 mph. Somebody made a mistake and this thing ruptured a seal. Once the steam has any means to escape, the rocket will break loose."

Mike, you had placed your chances of survival at thirty percent. Can you speak on the dangers inherent in rocketry?

So basically after that, I was going to launch again six months later at the same place just to try to make some money to cover my ass and pay bills and then that's when the accident happened.

A crew member was seriously injured and was flown by helicopter to the hospital in Tucson. Myself and another crew member were blown down to the ground by the thrust.

One of my crew members was actually on a part of the rocket. He had pulled himself up to look at a gauge, which he shouldn't have been up there.

His 200 and something pounds twisted something at the rear of the rocket that broke a seal. Once a pinhole of steam comes out, it'll just finally cut itself loose and that's what it did.

It snapped like four or five bolts and four pieces of chain and still went 3100 feet without me in it. It was horrifying.

I basically drove back home, physically, mentally and financially bankrupt.

So in your most recent jump in Amboy, n the footage from Noise TV on the canceled launch, you were explaining to people that you can't take any chances that it would literally make you into a skeleton, it would just strip the flesh off your ... if you're behind something like that.

Oh, yeah. That's why we didn't try to launch ... after the actuator failed the first time when I was in it, I had to get out of the rocket. The only other thing I could've done was beat on her from underneath, but you can't do that 'cause the steam would just blow the skin off from your bones.

It's coming out the speed of sound, 767 miles an hour. What do you think that'd do to you? It'd just ... it'd just destroy you.

It would be a water jet. Yeah, it would be a water jet, and a water jet will cut through metal.

So when you had to cancel that launch that day, when you climbed out, was there a danger it could've gone off as you were climbing out of the thing?

Yes. That is, it's possible. I really didn't feel that much when I was getting out of it because I figured we hadn't launched by now it wasn't gonna launch. But what we had thought may happen is once it started cooling down, the pressure started to drop overnight, then the actuator would work and would launch the rocket. We didn't know when I got there the next morning if the rocket would be still on the ramp, and luckily it was.

Fascinating. So that thing could have set off and killed you at that moment?

Oh, yeah, yeah. I really didn't think it was going to launch when I was getting out of it, of course. But you gotta realize we had already fired the gun, but the bullet had not left the barrel yet. That's the best way to explain this thing.

Yeah, I remember that was a pretty tense moment there.

Oh, it's about the most scared I've ever been my whole life. I was scared.

I remember the first time we spoke you said that you gave yourself a 30% chance of survival or something like that...

No, well my first launch in '14, yeah, it was leaking vapor that day and I had to climb over the vapor leak to get in the rocket. Then we couldn't actuate it. It took me, to make it happen it took both hands on this plunger bar to pull it. So I left the ramp not holding onto nothing that day. So I was taking four to seven G's that day with not holding onto nothing. So yeah, it's pretty horrifying.

Afterward then you were out for like three days, right?

Yes, yes, I hit really hard. I was injured. I was white for about a month after that. I lost all my color for about a month. I don't know what was going on. I think just from the shock that I took.

"Mad" Mike Hughes postponing his daring half-mile jump of Palo Duro Canyon:

"The best way to explain the power of this thing is you have caged the devil. When it takes off, there is no stopping it."

MAD MIKE VS THE BLM

Thanksgiving weekend was the date settled upon for the big launch. The news went out and the media focused its attention on this strange spectacle.

The common misperception that he was seeking to prove the Earth flat stuck. He was labeled as anti-science, crazy, and probably doomed.

The night before the launch, the Bureau of Land Management stepped in. He was too close to public land for them to allow him to continue. He moved the launch date forward to the next week, which turned out to be a good thing. The attention snowballed.

Mike was inundated with emails and phone calls. NoizeTV picked up on the story and did a live internet stream of the launch.

While the Bureau of Land Management had given him verbal permission more than a year prior to launch his rocket, however, a BLM spokesman said its local field office had no record of speaking to Hughes at the time.

So after seeing some news articles about the planned launch, a BLM representative reached out to Hughes with concerns.

The rocket launch, originally scheduled for the weekend of November 25, 2017, was delayed for lack of permits.

Even still, Mike's stunt did dominate the major newspaper headlines, including USA Today, The Drudge Report, and many others all over the world, making it one of the biggest news stories of 2017.

Hughes then rescheduled for December 2, 2017, and moved his launch pad 4 miles so that he could take off and land on private property.

Given that this launch was going for distance, there was a real possibility of it crossing into public property.

After moving the rocket, the BLM maintained he still needed to fill out permits. Hughes definitely stated the dispute would not stop him flying:

"I'm a daredevil. I'm not much for authority or rules."

THE REAL ROCKET MAN

The self-taught rocket scientist launched himself 1,875 feet into the air on March 24, 2018.

When asked if he feels vindicated he said after his successful launch and landing:

Mike: Well, somewhat. But I'll admit that people are still going to minimize what you've done. I've got people contacting saying, "Oh, you only went up 1875 feet. Hey, I could have taken an elevator. I could have walked up the tower in Dubai, I could have blown my drone for that", you know all that bullshit stuff.

You get back and say, "Guys, I launched a human being in a rocket launcher on the back of a motorhome. What do you not understand what's distorted about this?" See what I mean?

When asked if he would agree that the number of people who appreciate it outnumber the naysayers:

Mike: Oh yes.

MEDIA COVERAGE

It was just unbelievable. I was the second most shared and talked about the story on Facebook twice. Now that's saying a lot.

And I was the biggest news story once on the Associated Press, the biggest news story once on Google News and Yahoo News that I know of. I've appeared in newspapers everywhere. Even business newspapers: Forbes, Newsweek, the Washington Post. Even the China Communist newspaper wrote about me on the front page.

I was on seventeen national newspapers one day.

And there were several sides of that story besides the Flat Earth. For one, I launched this thing from a motorhome that I bought off Craigslist. It's the most bizarre part of the story. No one knew if it was going to hold up. I didn't know. I built this thing in my garage. I kept saying I was going to do it, and people kept saying, well, you're too old and this and that. And people don't understand that to do stuff like this, it takes a lifetime of experience and knowledge. This is what people did not understand.

Many people thought it was CGI until FOX went out there and said, "Yes, this is real. I'm touching it." I mean, that's how bizarre it is.

Because people cannot conceptualize that some guy can do this with his bare hands, has the balls to get into it, and it has the balls to say to everybody else that he's going to do it. They just can't because in their minds they think, "So I guess can't do it, so how can anyone else do it?"

THE DARE IN DAREDEVIL

How "Mad" Mike Hughes describes the Daredevil:

That's the guy that will roll the dice. In other words, it hasn't been scripted, it hasn't been practiced, it hasn't had a dummy put up in at once or it hasn't been mocked up in CGI.

It's like the Travis Pastrana thing at the Evel Live, which I heard is the one that one of the biggest shows that history channel had already this year. I tell people too, that is a $45,000 motorcycle made for racing and made for jumping that he is on.

And he had four of them. Now you've got to realize he's been practicing for months with speed guns and radar guns; he knows exactly how fast he's got to go. Each bike is set up for that particular type of jump.

He's riding a professional flat track racing machine. It is three times a motorcycle: thinner, lighter, better suspension and what Evel Knievel rode all those years ago.

So it's not even the same thing. The tires are better and it had special shocks and carbon fiber brakes in every one of those motorcycles.

So, you know, it was like after you did the first jump is like, well, he's done all three of them now. The Evel Live event was really one n the most worst produced things I've seen in my whole life.

Pastrana's a good motorcycle rider, yes. Probably average motorcycle racer. I don't think he ever raced that much as far as I know of. So he just found a niche and made it happen. And, and he's, he seems like a likable man that no one seemed like a great guy, you know, but you know, I tell people, you know, he couldn't cut it at Nascar. I was the first guy that said he was going to have. My quote was" he will have his ass handed to him in NASCAR", and people trashed me on the Internet when I said that.

You got to realize I'm one of the most innovative guys in the history of that sport. I have seen people's lives ruined. People with a lot more talent than that dude Travis Pastrana. I said you've got to realize the Indycar racer who won Indianapolis a couple of times, Dario Franchitti, could not drive one of these cars.

So you're telling me, Travis Pastrana, with no knowledge about setting cars up is going to do this? No, he's going to get his ass handed to him. Which is what happened.

He finally said, yeah, my critics were right. Well, of course, they were right. You don't know your ass from a hole in the ground, buddy.

You gotta go out there, you gotta learn the cars, and you've got to build him. Got to know how they work, you know?

They pumped a bunch of money in it and it was just, I couldn't take it. I watched the program and left. I came back home. I was in Vegas and I said, "this is a joke" when he came out wearing the Evel Knievel outfit... even put a cape on, and I'm going, "I'm not even buying this anymore." You know? Why would you do that stuff? Unless I get paid there is no reason to do it

All of this promotional posters had pictures, had black leathers with stars and stripes to the front and he comes out and the day the jumps with these white leathers like Evel Knievel. I thought, "this is bullshit." He sure spent money on pyrotechnics.

POLITICAL ASPIRATIONS

Statements such as: "Everything about our lives is how we perceive things. The money in your pocket right now, you perceive it to be real. It's not. It's monopoly money. With debt attached to it," may not paint a rosy picture of the world, but according to Mike, we already have answers to all of our problems:

We have all the answers to fix all the problems. The problem with that statement is there's no money in fixing problems. Only managing them. That's why we have private-run prisons.

I really would like every alphabet agency to go away. We're not letting them into the state. FEMA, CIA, FBI could not come into the state because they are criminal enterprises.

Every living president would be under indictment in this state. If you want to bring them to the state, I don't care if it's a bounty hunter. I don't care what it is. You bring them here, we'll put them on trial. They all go to war crimes and treason.

It's just bizarre how we're doing things. You've got to get rid of all these unions. We don't need unions anymore.

This state, California, should be, making its own cars. We should make your own cell phones. We should be making everything. The bullshit thing is how much there is made in Vietnam and brought over here and we were killing them 50 years ago. Now they're making our Levis.

The thing is we as a society have been hijacked by secret societies and BAR attorneys. There are some people now that have come up with the argument or with the facts that the Constitution was hijacked all by freemasons. They were supposed to have penned the Articles of Confederation, which is what we were under at the time.

That's when they came up with this Constitution, which is actually a charter. A corporate charter. Not really a constitution. It was Freemasons who basically hijacked that. No one voted on that. What, 13 guys? 14? They said, "That's what we're going to do now?"

When no one signs off or nothing and it's not done under full disclosure and everything and it's all null and void.

The problem is people don't have all the facts. I think the easiest way to describe this stuff, even with flat Earth, even with political stuff and presidential races is everything is a puzzle and this puzzle that we're given about life is always missing pieces. I don't care if it's 9/11, Sandy Hook, the flat Earth, Donald Trump, certainly Hillary Clinton and Barack Obama, man. Half the pieces were missing from that fucker's puzzle.

His thoughts on the Military:

We invent our own enemies. That's what we do. You have to. It's like 9/11. We invented an enemy. Of course, you're aware of that Osama Bin Laden thing. We were funding him at one time. We start and fund our own enemies. We've been doing that for decades.

It's psychopathic is what it is, but you've got to have an enemy and then you've got to get people behind it. There it is. People don't do their research. You know how many people have told me they thought Condoleezza Rice would be a good candidate for president or Colin Powell? I said, "You know those people lied about the thing in Iraq." They initially said there wasn't. A year later saying there was. Colin Powell is a thirty-third-degree freemason supposedly.

I've had people tell me Newt Gingrich would be a good candidate. I say, "Are you kidding me?" I say, "He's a freemason and he's knee deep in Fanny May's Freddie Mac bullshit." These people stay around forever. They never go away.

COMMON LAW

I think the court system is the way is to start changing things.

I do not recognize bar attorneys, they cannot speak in my court and my case, my claim, and I say basically, you know, the court I, the paperwork, it is not the building.

All these courts are courts of record and are supposed to proceed under Common Law and that'll say that is per article six, section one, the California constitution.

And I said we will not recognize latin here. We're going to speak American English preferably funding Merriam diction dictionary a from 1823 to 1828. People's heads were spinning.

Look at the California constitution. All courts are courts of record and of course, their record is to proceed under common law. So I may and I told the judge that I'm the only one in the building doing anything lawful right now. Everything else is fraud.

Common law is the law of the land. In other words, there was no crime committed unless a man or a man or woman or their property has been harmed.

And that is the law. For example, if you go five miles an hour over the speed limit sign, which is a and advisory sign, what it is, it's not even for you. It's for people in commerce. All these tickets are bogus. All this stuff is bogus. But all this stuff is morphed into what it is today.

It's all outside the scope of authority. No one has a delegation of authority. No one, not the judges, not the cops, no one, because that had to come from Congress.

It's all fraud. Just as much as the money in your pocket right now. You cannot convince cops that code and statute is not law.

You know, I've told these military people, "You know, you're not fighting for my freedom for anyone else's freedom. You're fighting for defense contractors' profits. That's what you're fighting for. You are a pawn. And man, that makes people crazy.

I've already put my congressman on notice. I will follow charges against him on treason. Today was his last day to get in touch with me. If not, within 45 days, I will file treason charges against you in common law court.

And I do believe in public hangings, also.

Once you start hanging these guys, it all stops. It all stops. Because you know what? There are about 8,000 people that are really kind of in control of things. So now, you're thinking, Well, if you get rid of those guys, you have to probably get rid of the two or three guys underneath them also that's ready to step in. So, that's 24,000 people that you gotta off really quickly. So it is better just to put some of these people that are already retired, that are still living, charge them the stuff, and just hang them.

We'll put the military tribunal court in some weird island somewhere. Maybe, take them back to Jekyll Island where all this bullshit started. The creature from Jekyll, take them there and hang them, right there, where all the bullshit started with all the fake money.

PROTESTING MASS MEDIA

Mike's views on sports entertainment:

Men, quit following these stupid sports teams.
Men, do something else with your time and your life
it. That drives me batshit crazy. It really does. I mean,
I tried two years ago to watch the Superbowl. I'm at a
bar by myself. I wanted to have one beer. I'm going to
watch it. I watched the halftime and before the damn
thing even starts there prayed the military, which is
what they do and militaries, part of everything. You
know what I mean? And, and then they pushed
George HW Bush out across the football field and
people are standing up cheering in the bar.

So I'm saying to the lady that was sitting next to
me, I'm going, "You know, the guy's a criminal. He's a
pedophile, you know, he called for a New World

Order. Why aren't people standing up and saying this?" and she looked at me like I was from outer space.

I said, "This guy is a criminal and a pedophile. Why is anybody cheering this idiot?"

So I got up and left. I couldn't deal with anymore. Anytime you see some big event, it always has the military involved. The big flags, you know, all this pageantry, the pledge of allegiance. It's all bullshit.

In fact, I think "support your troops" actually came from the CIA. I think they came up with that bullshit also. We've all had a red, white and blue dildo stuck up our ass since day one.

I left. I couldn't deal with it. These people not knowing how big a crime syndicate the Bush family is, it's a crime syndicate.

If it wasn't for the internet coming on '95, we'd already be in New World Order. Everybody would already be chipped.

CRITICS AND NAYSAYERS

Mike's thoughts on risk vs reward, and ignoring the critics.

Well, you gotta realize I've had three or four sponsors back away because of Flat Earth.

In fact, Arai Helmets does not want anything else to do with me. So, in fact, they want all the decals taken off, patches off my uniform, whatever. And that came from Japan, that's what I was told. That word came out of Japan. It just freaked them out. They don't care about the media. I mean, that's how stupid people are.

I had an old sponsor, he gave me some money once. Soon as the flat earth got on it, he started bitching out saying I was embarrassing him and I pulled everything off the website, off the rocket. He threatened to sue me and all kinds of stuff. It's, yeah, it got ugly.

The Washington Post commented on one of Mike's delayed launches:

"But Saturday marked Hughes's third aborted launch since he declared himself a flat-earther last year and announced a multipart plan to fly to space by the end of 2018 so he could prove astronauts have been lying about the shape of the planet.

The Washington Post, like many news outlets, covered Hughes's plan. In retrospect, we admit, there was never any chance he'd pull it off."

That particular launch was canceled. Hughes blamed technical difficulties, likely a bad O-ring. Of course, Mike later proved them wrong, as he said he would.

Even retired NASA astronaut Jerry Linenger chimed in:

"I hope he doesn't blow something up," said, as Mr. Hughes' plans captured widespread attention. "Rocketry, as our private space companies found out, isn't as easy as it looks," he said.

After the canceled launch of February 2nd, Hughes climbed out of the rocket to face the cameras. He scratched his head.

"I pulled the plunger five different times," Hughes said. "I considered beating on the rocket nozzle from the underneath side. But you can't get anyone under there. It'll kill you. It'll scald you to death. It'll blow the skin and muscle off your bones."

RENAISSANCE MAN OR MADMAN?

Now that he pulled off the world's greatest daredevil stunt, Mike discusses his future plans:

He announced a Rocket Race in Las Vegas, Nevada for August 2019:

Johnny Knoxville Travis Pastrana, you know, I call people out because I believe, from what I've done, I'm the top daredevil in the world.

King of the daredevils.

On his speedboat:

It stays just barely contact with the water. Mine will have five contact points on the water. There are certain angles you do and areas that it rides on.

Basically, the speed record on water is the world's most dangerous speed record for a lot of reasons.

If something goes bad, it goes bad very quickly and very badly. There's no way to save one if it gets sideways, there's no way of saving. It's gonna go, it's gonna tumble, it's gonna start slinging parts off the boat. Then it will start slinging parts inside your body. That's what happens, it starts throwing organs around, all kinds of ... the last four out of six guys, I believe, that's attempted this record have died.

Mike's thoughts on Flat Earth:

What would you say your message would be with regards to flat Earth?

Just research it and draw your own conclusions. Do whatever test you can do. The thing is with me, I know and a lot of other people know that everything is a lie. This is what makes it more able for me to grab on to this thing, that this may possibly be true. I am more prone to think the world is just motionless, okay? That's what I believe. I really believe the world is just motionless, stationary."

His thoughts on Global Warming:

I think CO2 has always been around. I think the ice age ... We've had probably two or three of them. My concern is just the poisoning of the water because that's when everything comes to a screeching halt, okay? If there's no water, everything dies and it goes away. The whole plastic thing. It's just ludicrous. We're still driving automobiles powered by petroleum products. It's absolutely asinine. It's asinine.

I think, honestly, electromagnetism is where we need to go. There have been motors developed over the years that people have been threatened or disappeared. Honestly, you can run your car engine on an air compressor. That's probably what we should do initially.

With the vehicle, you could run it off an air compressor. We've never brought any of those cars here.

People have built a biosphere to grow plants in Nebraska and the heat is being piped from eight feet under where its 52 degrees and that is what heats the thing during the wintertime.

There are so many different ways to do things. Everyone should have a garden on the roof. Give the kids something to do at night; to learn about gardening, about nutrition, and to learn about all of this done. Most of all, put down those video games.

Now it's going into AI, and they're going into virtual reality and I don't know if it's all about escaping the world, but the problem is, these games are violent, and we already have too much violence. And it's planned. Same with social media. It's planned to divide people further.

GOVERNOR MICHAEL HUGHES

I saw that there were a lot of kids at the rocket launch watching you go up. What would you say to the children of today:

Mike: Those kids were looking at me like I was Superman that day when I got on that rocket, which I was. They saw a real-life superman that day. When I go up into space, and people were going to gather to talk to me, on the way up there... Historic.

I built this by my brainpower, my research, my bare hands. At the end of the day, I still launched more humans in rockets than Elon Musk has. People actually believe that he launched a Tesla into space. I mean, that's bizarre. That never happened.

His thoughts on the Mainstream Media:

Mike: They're just being told what to say, what to promote. In fact, you can go to a bunch of these channels, the anchor people are saying the same thing on each network. They're reading a script. That's been proven.

They're reading a script.

There's a guy named Max Igan who I've been listening to now for a little while. This guy's from Australia. He knew as a young man thing were not right. He said, "at age 4 I knew something wasn't right". How could people own land? He became a musician just to get away, to get on the fringe of society to travel and live a different lifestyle under the table, cash, all this kind of stuff.

I listen to this guy a lot and he says "You've got to realize, everything, all the languages, all the history, has been tainted and changed." He says, "You're telling me the only two things that haven't been tainted and changed and kicked around is the Quran and the Bible. Are you serious? You better believe that both those books have been altered."

A lot of people would not allow them to accept that. People think that honestly there was a massive flood and they put animals inside of an arc and floated around for 40 days. People believe that.

His thoughts on biblical literalism?

Mike: Who knows who approved the books. You can go back to the Flavian family, the Romans that invented Christianity. I don't know, I wasn't there. See what I mean? I don't know.

It's just like the Flat Earth. I don't know. I'm just kind of watching what I've researched and looked at the stars in the same place every night and it's kind of led me down that path. Everything has been tainted. The Incas, the Aztecs, their history. All these genocides. We were never taught in school that we killed 96% of the indigenous people.

Mike on Experts:

Mike: The problem is...they have to have all the answers. I have admitted several times I do not have all the answers, and it's impossible to have all the answers.

Who says you're an expert? You know what I mean? Some scientific community that's being funded, and if you don't go along with the status quo they'll pull your funding?

You look around at all the chiropractors from the 20's to the 40's and the 50's and all the homeopathics, they're still going to kill the homeopathic physicians. It is absolutely bizarre.

I'll tell you some things that I will do if I can pull this thing off for governor. I will mandate that every automobile that is sold in California within two years has to have a fuel vaporizer system that will double or triple the fuel mileage. Retro kits for everyone else. They will start building ethanol from fungi spore.

Ethanol from fungi spore?:

Mike: Yes, that's already been proven it can be done. In fact, that guy is in I think Bellingham, WA. He did a TED speech about it. It's very interesting how fungi and mold spores can save the world. Yeah, we have all the answers to fix all the problems.

I don't care if it's fiberglass homes for the homeless, to hemp concrete, and no more building anything unless it's got hemp in it. It's going to have hemp in the concrete or whatever. We don't need lime, we don't need all these chemicals and certainly, I will not allow in this state. They will not be allowed in this state.

I will not allow the IRS to come here and tax anyone in the state of California unless you're a business. Individuals, no one will have to pay taxes. I will not allow any employees to take out federal taxes. They can take me to court.

Mike on Drug Cartels:

Why are we not going out to the drug cartels in Mexico? We could shut him down at 45 to 60 days. We could do that.

Why aren't we dragging the Mexican President into court here as a terrorist? They are terrorists. We're allowing invasion of an army.

On Defense Spending:

A couple weeks ago, I told a military guy, "If you don't know the PNAC document is, then you don't know what's going on about war, because that describes all the wars. And they're all Israel's wars. Why are we supporting Israel? Why are we giving Israel eleven million dollars a day? Why are we giving NASA fifty-three million dollars a day? And why are we spending eight point three million dollars an hour on the military per hour?

You think about those numbers for a second. We have homelessness in this country. We could pay off everyone's mortgages. And we can eliminate sales tax. Everyone would actually be free.

Could we get by with just a reserve army? Can we get by with closing every base in the world and bringing everyone back? You're protecting your own borders and solving your own problems. Can we agree that for four years hit a reset button, because nothing else is working?

Do not elect any more bar attorneys. Do not elect any more Republicans or Democrats. Let's do everything totally different. Try that four years.

Mike's Political Platform:

Mike: I don't know, I'm just one guy. I'm one man.

It's the raw truth. Like I said before, I want my coffee and I don't want any whipped cream on top of it, you know what I mean? I just want this raw truth. I just wish--if Trump was really the guy that everyone he was going to be, he would have already done a live Internet pay-per-view and laid just out everything. All the frauds, all the JFK stuff, all the 9/11, and he has not done that. He has not done that. It's like he's swore allegiance to some Golden Ball in Saudi Arabia. Remember he had his hands on that glowing ball?

On his part statements about disbanding various government agencies:

Mike: I would not allow any outside agencies in the state. None. They're all terrorists. CIA and FBI are terrorist organizations. They find drugs, they find terrorism. The FBI- Osama Bin Laden was never the main suspect for 9/11. You know that, don't you?

We're calling the FBI or any kind of military intelligence from the 1998 bombing. That's why he was a suspect, but never for 9/11. And very few people know that.

Mike: Well, we're kind of taught that. We're taught in school through programming centers to never question authority, and to follow in line, just stay behind the person in front of you and don't ask questions. That's the way we're taught. We're taught to ridicule anyone that questions that.

FUTURE PLANS

I want to build a sanctuary for foster kids, injured animals, or animals that need a home. I want to do a sanctuary for both.

I have found some land. It's very expensive. But I'm thinking with my tour coming out, hopefully, I'll donate all of the proceeds for that to go to a sanctuary.

I just want to inspire kids. That is the future.

POLITICAL PLATFORM

- Public Hangings
- Close the border, Build the wall
- Deport all illegal immigrants
- Eliminate taxes
- Eliminate gun restrictions
- Ban all BAR attorneys
- End the war on drugs
- Stop all fires
- End poverty forever
- STOP Monsanto
- END HOA

- Eliminate minimum wage
- Eliminate traffic
- Wage war on all politics as usual
- Stop chemtrails
- No fluoride in the water
- Expose the Flat Earth
- Getting Woman out of the workplace and bringing back traditional home values
- Single income household
- 2 Genders ONLY!

MIKE'S PROPOSED STUNT/EXPERIMENT

-- Originally published in The Flat Earth Report, 11.15.2018, Conference Edition

Experiments can be derided and ignored; a stunt commands attention. Especially a death-defying all-time record-setting daredevil stunt.

Let's be honest: the Bedford Level Experiment made the case for a Flat Earth. As do many other observations and incontrovertible facts. So why do the people of the world still believe it to be a spinning ball in space?
Because they exist in a self-reinforcing echo chamber that is saturated by space program propaganda. The only way for an experiment to succeed in breaking the spell is for it to be unignorable.

And if unignorable is what you need, "Mad" Mike Hughes is your man.

His previous stunt is still going viral on the Internet. You know, the steam-powered rocket jump which made the covers of seventeen national newspapers?

So, what's his plan?

Simple. He's going to top the famed Red Bull Jump, which was supposed to be from the "edge of space", but fell far short of the accepted 62-mile altitude, delineating the true "edge of space". At twenty miles, his jump was noteworthy, but not a useful experiment from a Flat Earth vs Round Earth standpoint. It simply wasn't high enough. It received plenty of publicity, as all good daredevil stunts do.

"Mad" Mike Hughes, however, plans to soar up to the Karman Line itself, sixty-two miles above, by way of balloon-rocket hybrid.

"Life is full of compromises without compromising yourself."

REFERENCES

Loulla-Mae Eleftheriou-Smith (27 November 2017). "Flat-Earther 'Mad' Mike Hughes forced to delay the launch of the homemade rocket". The Independent. Retrieved 29 November 2017."'I Don't Believe In Science,' Says Flat-Earther Set To Launch Himself In Own Rocket". NPR.org. Retrieved 29 November 2017.

"Self-Taught Rocket Scientist Mad Mike Hughes Plans to Launch Over Ghost Town". NBC4 Washington. Associated Press. Retrieved 29 November 2017.

"A flat-Earther's plan to launch himself in a homemade rocket has been postponed — again". chicagotribune.com. Retrieved 29 November 2017.

""Mad" Mike built a rocket so he can jump the Grand Canyon of Texas". Ars Technica. Retrieved 29 November 2017.

"Longest limousine ramp jump". Guinness World Records. Retrieved 26 March 2018.

a b c Wang, Amy B.; Selk, Avi (24 November 2017). "A flat-Earther's plan to launch himself in a homemade rocket just hit a speed bump". Washington Post. Retrieved 29 November 2017.

"Self-taught rocket scientist 'Mad' Mike Hughes blasts off into California sky". Retrieved 25 March 2018.

"Flat-Earther's steam-powered rocket lofts him 1,875 feet up into Mojave Desert sky". latimes.com. Associated Press. 2018. Retrieved 26 March 2018.

"Self-taught rocket scientist eyes new launch date in Calif". Las Vegas Review-Journal. 28 November 2017. Retrieved 29 November 2017.

Dow, Mike (13 December 2017). "'Mad' Mike Hughes – limo driver turned rocket man". The Maine Edge. Retrieved 10 January 2018.

Selk, Avi; Wang, Amy B. (6 February 2018). "Analysis | A flat-earther finally tried to fly away. His rocket didn't even ignite". Washington Post. Retrieved 7 February 2018.

Chiara Giordano (25 March 2018). "Flat-earther blasts off in homemade rocket in bid to reassure himself world is shaped 'like a Frisbee'". The Independent. Retrieved 25 March 2018.

"Why you don't need a rocket to prove the planet is round". Newsweek. 28 November 2017. Retrieved 30 November 2017.

PHOTO GALLERY

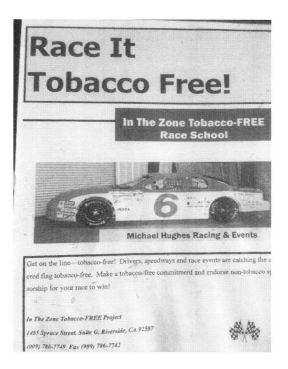

This is a picture of a car that was part of my racing and driving school that was at the Orange Show Speedway in San Bernardino.

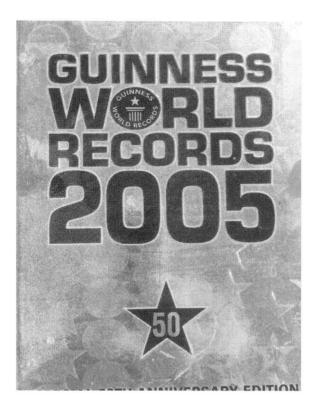

Guinness record book that the limo jump record
appears in

(Mike preparing the Liberty Rocket for launch)

(Information Overload interviewing Mike)

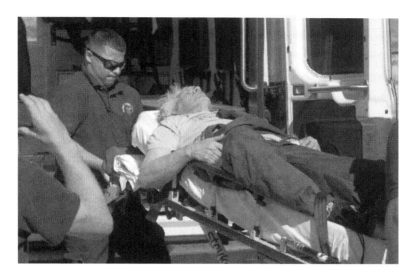

(After the launch EMT checked Mike for injuries)

Michael Hughes
2953 South Vineyard #126
Ontario
CA
91762
United States

Claim ID: 38518
Membership Number: 37177

18 December 2003

Dear Michael,

We are pleased to inform you that you have been successful in setting a new Guinness World Record. A certificate to commemorate this achievement is enclosed.

Details of this record have been entered into our records database for potential use in future Guinness World Records publications and products. Although this certificate does not automatically guarantee an entry our managing editors consider all new records for use as required.

Once again welcome to the very select brand of Guinness World Records holders!

Yours sincerely,

Ann Collins

Guinness World Records Limited
338 Euston Road London NW1 3BD • Telephone +44 (0)20 7891 4567
Fax. +44 (0)20 7891 4561 • e-mail crm@guinnessworldrecords.com
Registered in England, Company number 541295. VAT No. GB 227 3091 92
Registered Office: Maple House, 149 Tottenham Court Road, London W1T 7BN United Kingdom
A HiT Entertainment company

Man Plans Saturday Launch
Homemade Steam Powered Rocket

Newsrooms were incredulous and fascinated by the stunt.

Made in the USA
Las Vegas, NV
14 November 2020